Study Guide

Seven Simple Secrets

This Study Guide provides thought-provoking questions and easy-to-implement activities to help you apply the concepts in the bestselling book, *Seven Simple Secrets, Second Edition*. Step by step, it walks you through considering what you've read, taking action to implement the secrets and strategies of highly effective teachers, and sharing your learning with others—all leading to improved teaching and learning!

You can work on the guide independently, in book study groups, with professional learning communities (PLCs), and in professional development sessions. This guide will help you to take full advantage of the seven secrets and implement them immediately in your own classroom!

Annette Breaux is an internationally-renowned speaker and bestselling author of numerous books on teaching, learning, and leading. She is best known for her work in the areas of classroom management and new-teacher induction.

Todd Whitaker is a leading presenter in the field of education and the author of more than 30 books for teachers and school leaders. He is a professor of educational leadership at Indiana State University in Terre Haute, Indiana.

Nancy Satterfield is a retired assistant superintendent for assessment and professional development for the Henderson County Schools in Kentucky. She is currently working as a grant writer for the school district.

Study Guide

Seven Simple Secrets

What the BEST Teachers Know and Do!

Second Edition

Annette Breaux and Todd Whitaker
Nancy Satterfield

Routledge
Taylor & Francis Group

NEW YORK AND LONDON

Second edition published 2015
by Routledge
711 Third Avenue, New York, NY 10017

and by Routledge
2 Park Square, Milton Park, Abingdon, Oxon, OX14 4RN

Routledge is an imprint of the Taylor & Francis Group, an informa business

First edition published by Eye On Education 2006

Library of Congress Cataloging-in-Publication Data

Breaux, Annette L.
   Study guide, seven simple secrets : what the BEST teachers know and do! / by
Annette Breaux, Todd Whitaker, and Nancy Satterfield. — Second edition.
    pages cm
  1. Teaching—Handbooks, manuals, etc.   2. Classroom management—Handbooks, manuals, etc.
I. Whitaker, Todd, 1959–   II. Satterfield, Nancy.   III. Routledge study guides.   IV. Title.
   LB1025.3.B7435 2014
   371.102—dc23   2014003032

ISBN: 978-1-138-78362-1 (pbk)
ISBN: 978-1-315-76858-8 (ebk)

Typeset in Palatino
by Apex CoVantage, LLC

Printed and bound in the United States of America by Sheridan Books, Inc. (a Sheridan Group Company).

Contents

Introduction

This study guide will help you reflect on the ideas in *Seven Simple Secrets, Second Edition,* so that you can apply them in your own classroom.

For ease of use, this study guide mirrors the structure of the main book. It is divided into seven chapters, one for each secret. Each chapter is then divided into the seven parts found within each secret. You can read each chapter in a sequential manner or select the secret on which you would like to focus.

Throughout the guide, you'll find questions that ask you to Reflect, Take Action, and Share. As you **reflect** on what you've read, **take action** to implement the suggestions in the book, and **share** your learning with others, you will become more confident and effective. As a result, student engagement will increase and student achievement will rise. Isn't that our ultimate goal?

We wish you your most exciting and rewarding school year ever!

Secret One:
The Secret of Planning

Part One: How to Have a Great Plan

The most effective teachers know that to have a great lesson—you need to PLAN a great lesson. This section of the book reveals how and why to prioritize lesson planning.

Reflect:

1. In your own words, describe why lesson planning is so important.

2. Do you set aside a particular block of time each day to plan your lessons? If not, how might you rearrange your schedule to allow specific time for planning?

3. What are the key components to a good lesson plan?

4. Do you currently include all the key components in your lessons? If not, what can you do to improve? Explain.

✓ Take Action:

5. List two ways you can be more efficient and effective in your planning.

6. Think of a lesson you taught recently that wasn't as well planned as you'd like. Using what you've learned, make a few minor adjustments to improve that plan.

💬 Share:

7. Take part in a lesson swap where you and a colleague exchange lesson plans and provide feedback to one another. What did you learn from him or her that can be applied to future lessons?

Part Two: How to Over-plan

The most effective teachers, as part of their secret to successful planning, always **over-plan**.

 Reflect:

1. Have you ever planned an activity that didn't take as long as you had anticipated? Describe where your timing was off, how you filled the time (if you did), and how students reacted.

✓ Take Action:

2. Add a couple of "over-planning activities" to one of your upcoming lesson plans. Tip: Plan quality activities as opposed to time fillers.

💬 Share:

3. Share your over-planning ideas with a colleague and ask for feedback.

Part Three: How to Manage Your Time

It's all about teaching in small bites! Some of the most effective teachers plan their lessons in **5-minute segments**.

💡 Reflect:

1. How might it benefit both you and your students if you plan in brief segments? Explain.

✓ Take Action:

2. Using 5-minute segments, plan an upcoming lesson. Teach the lesson and reflect on how this approach worked for you and your students.

💬 Share:

3. Share the lesson plan and its results with a colleague and/or with your team. Discuss any changes/improvements you noticed in student engagement.

Part Four: How to Be Flexible

The most effective teachers know that **flexibility** is a must in planning. After all, "the best-laid plans" often don't go as planned! This section focuses on how to cope with interruptions during your day.

Reflect:

1. Do you consider yourself flexible when it comes to accommodating interruptions to your daily routine? Explain.

2. Why is flexibility a MUST in teaching?

✓ Take Action:

3. Start noticing interruptions and how you react to them. Jot a few of these down, along with a few ideas for handling them effectively.

4. What would you suggest to the administration as possible ways to minimize interruptions in your school? Work with colleagues to come up with three or four suggestions.

⌬ Share:

5. Share your tips from question 4 with a team or school leader.

Part Five: How to Make Objectives Clear

Making **objectives** clear is vital to helping students succeed. Students must have a clear understanding of what they will learn during a lesson.

💡 Reflect:

1. Review your lesson plans from the past week. Did you clearly identify your objectives for the lesson? Were students *aware* of the objectives?

2. Describe the difference between lesson activities and lesson objectives. Give two examples of each.

✓ Take Action:

3. Write a lesson plan with clearly-stated objectives. Also determine how you will share these objectives with students at the beginning of the lesson.

💬 Share:

4. Share your lesson plan with a colleague. Better yet, consider contributing it to a lesson plan website so that you can share it with an even wider audience!

Part Six: How to Promote Activity

We know that whoever is doing the "**doing**" is doing the learning! In your classroom, are the students "doing" the work or are you—the teacher—the person most actively engaged?

▽ Reflect:

1. Explain what the phrase "doing most of the doing" means.

2. How might you transfer more of the "doing" to students? Be specific.

✓ Take Action:

3. Plan a lesson with activities to ensure that students remain actively engaged. Be sure to incorporate higher-order thinking in discussions and activities. Teach the lesson and reflect on how it worked.

💬 Share:

4. Tell a colleague how the lesson went. Discuss ideas for improvement if needed.

Part Seven: How to Be Proactive

Being **proactive** means anticipating typical problems and warding them off before they occur. This section of the book uses the examples of Ms. Reactive and Ms. Proactive to illustrate the importance of being proactive when planning lessons and activities for your students.

💡 Reflect:

1.   How would you describe yourself—reactive or proactive? Explain.

✓ Take Action:

2.   Make a list of tips and strategies you can use to be more proactive in the classroom.

💬 Share:

3.   Share your list from question 2 with colleagues. Ask them to contribute additional strategies.

Secret One Summary Checklist

The following statements summarize the strategies from Secret One. Read each statement and check the column that best represents where you would rank yourself. Reflect on where you can improve.

1 = Rarely or never
2 = Sometimes
3 = On a consistent basis

STRATEGIES	1	2	3
1. My lesson objectives are clear and measurable.			
2. My lessons reflect my students' interests and involvement in their learning.			
3. I follow the 60/40 rule.			
4. I over-plan my lessons.			
5. I plan lessons in small segments.			
6. I am flexible and able to adapt to changes in my routines.			
7. I am able to focus on things I CAN control and let go of those I can't.			
8. My objectives are supported by appropriate activities that engage students.			
9. I am a proactive teacher.			

Secret Two:
The Secret of Classroom Management

Part One: What an Effective Teacher's Classroom Looks Like

This section of the book describes what can be observed in both effective and ineffective classrooms.

💡 Reflect:

1. Think back to a former teacher who would fall into the "less-effective" category. Describe what that classroom "looked like."

2. Now think about a former teacher who would fall into the "highly-effective" category. Describe what occurred in that classroom.

3. Which description do you feel best describes your classroom? Would others agree? Explain.

✓ Take Action:

4. Identify two or three "effective teaching" characteristics from the list (page 23 in the book) that you could better incorporate into your teaching. Practice using these for two weeks. At the end of those two weeks, make a short list describing your successes.

 Share:

5. Share your list from question 4 with your team or a colleague and have them share theirs with you. You'll all benefit!

Part Two: How to Distinguish Between Rules and Procedures

A **rule** is something that regulates serious student misbehavior. A **procedure** is simply a way that you expect something to be done.

💡 Reflect:

1. Do you have clearly-stated classroom rules for student behavior? How were these rules developed and communicated to students?

2. Have you established procedures for how you expect things to be done in your classroom? How were they developed and communicated to students?

3. How often do you typically have to enforce the rules each day?

4. Are you consistent with the implementation of your procedures? Describe what you do to ensure that your procedures are followed.

✓ Take Action:

5. If necessary, rewrite your rules and procedures to make sure they are phrased in a positive way. Can any of your rules be reframed as procedures?

💬 Share:

6. Share your revised rules and procedures with your colleagues and ask for feedback. Get some additional ideas by asking each member of your team to share a procedure that works especially well for him or her. You might also start a thread on your favorite social media site asking teachers to share their most effective classroom procedures.

Part Three: How to Establish Rules and Procedures

Effective teachers have very few **rules.**

💡 Reflect:

1. This section of the book describes the process that effective teachers use when establishing both rules and procedures. Are these steps similar to how you establish your own rules and procedures? Describe the similarities and differences.

2. Are you consistent with the implementation of your rules and procedures? Explain.

✓ Take Action:

3. List a few ways you want to improve upon the implementation of rules and procedures in your classroom.

💬 **Share:**

4. Meet with your team and share your method of establishing classroom rules and procedures. Compare your method with those of your team members.

Part Four: How to Provide Reminders and Practice

In this section of the book, you read about what to do when students do *not* follow rules and procedures.

💡 Reflect:

1. In your own classroom, what usually happens when students don't follow a rule? How do you react?

2. What do you typically do when a student does not follow a procedure?

✓ Take Action:

3. Create a short practice script of what you might say to students who need reminders about following a rule. Now do the same for procedures.

💬 **Share:**

4. Share your script from question 3 with a colleague and get suggestions for making it even more effective, if necessary. Use language from your script the next time a student does not follow a rule or procedure.

Part Five: How to Teach from Bell to Bell

The busier students are, the less time they have to misbehave. And the busier they remain, the better their achievement!

💡 Reflect:

1. Do you teach from bell to bell, or do your students have occasional free time either at the beginning of class, following activities, or at the end of class?

✓ Take Action:

2. Create a list of five bell-ringers (also known as lesson starters, warm-ups, bell-work, do-nows, etc.) that you could use to get students working right away.

3. Create a list of activities you could use at the end of class if your lesson ends early. (Tip: This could also be a good opportunity to use an exit slip or some other method of formative assessment to help you determine how well students learned the day's lesson.)

💬 **Share:**

4. Share your bell-ringer activities on a social media site and ask other teachers in your subject area to share their ideas. If you prefer, simply share with a colleague or two.

Part Six: How to Discipline Proactively

Less-effective teachers run around putting out fires while more-effective teachers practice fire prevention!

💡 Reflect:

1. Which of the two teachers described in this chapter would you say best represents your discipline approach? Explain.

✓ Take Action:

2. If you are more reactive than proactive, what steps can you take to change that?

3. If you feel you are already proactive, what can you do to be even more proactive?

💬 Share:

4. Discuss, with your team or a colleague, ways of being more proactive.

Part Seven: How *Not* to Be a Screamer

It is *never* appropriate or effective to yell or scream at a student.

💡 Reflect:

1. In any school, students and parents can always identify the teachers who are known for raising their voices in an attempt to control their students. The most effective teachers, however, do just the opposite. They remain calm, cool, and collected—and they always deal with students in a professional manner. How would your students and their parents rate you if asked about your tone of voice and your professionalism in dealing with students?

2. Reflect on the following: "The more out of control the student—the more in control an effective teacher must be." Describe a time when a student lost control in your classroom. How did you handle it?

✓ Take Action:

3. Come up with three to five strategies to help defuse an out-of-control student.

💬 Share:

4. Share your list with a colleague or two and ask them to share their own
    strategies.

Secret Two Summary Checklist

The following statements summarize the strategies from Secret Two. Read each statement and check the box that best applies. Wherever you've checked "no," set a goal for yourself to improve in that area.

STRATEGIES	YES	NO
1. My classroom is organized with "a place for everything, and everything in its place."		
2. I am enthusiastic and filled with excitement when I teach.		
3. I have clearly-established rules and procedures in my classroom, and my students understand what is expected of them.		
4. I have consistent consequences for broken rules.		
5. I have procedures for just about everything.		
6. I try to discipline proactively so I don't have to put out fires later.		
7. I teach from bell to bell so students don't have time to misbehave.		
8. I rarely have to stop teaching in order to re-establish control.		
9. I maintain my composure and never yell at my students, no matter what they do.		
10. I am in control of myself and of my classroom.		

Secret Three:
The Secret of Instruction

Part One: How to Teach for Real Life

The most effective teachers define **real-life teaching** as relating the skills they teach to the real lives of their students.

💡 Reflect:

1. This section of the book describes two different approaches to teaching pronouns. Do you identify with either approach? If so, which one?

2. Reflect on a lesson you taught recently and determine whether you made a real-life connection for students. If not, how might you have made the connection?

✓ Take Action:

3. Select one new skill you will be teaching next week. Plan an exciting way to connect this lesson and its activities to your students' lives.

💬 **Share:**

4. After you teach the lesson from question 3, share the results with your colleagues. You might even choose to share with parents, as part of a classroom newsletter, the exciting, real-world learning that's occurring in your classroom!

Part Two: How to Ensure Active Student Involvement

In this section of the book, the authors relate **active learning** to intentional or meaningful learning.

⚲ Reflect:

1. When you look at your own teaching, do you observe students engaged in meaningful, intentional learning? Explain.

✓ Take Action:

2. Revise an upcoming lesson to include more active student involvement. (Each of us can improve in this area.)

⤷ Share:

3. Do a web search for new ideas to increase active student involvement. Share the ideas with other teachers at your school or with your social media followers.

Part Three: How to Ensure Success for All Students

Effective teachers refuse to believe that there is any such thing as a student who is incapable of succeeding and achieving.

💡 Reflect:

1. What are your thoughts about the introductory statement above?

2. Think of a time (in your own schooling or in teaching) when you experienced trouble learning or mastering something. How would you have wanted others to have reacted or to have helped you? How might you apply that to your own teaching?

✓ Take Action:

3. How can you better teach each student at his or her own level? Come up with a list of four or five strategies.

⬭ **Share:**

4. Share your strategies with team members and other school colleagues. Post your ideas on a blog or on the school's internal drive so that other educators can benefit.

Part Four: How to Incorporate Technology Effectively

Today's students live in a technologically-advanced world. This part of the book discusses strategies for effectively incorporating **technology in your lessons.**

Reflect:

1. In general, describe your comfort level with the use of technology in the classroom.

2. Describe how you currently use technology to enhance your teaching.

3. On a scale of 1–10, how effectively do you feel you are using technology in your classroom?

✓ Take Action:

4. Come up with two new ways to incorporate technology even more effectively in your teaching.

5. Visit teacher websites, education blogs, or online learning communities to find new ideas for using technology effectively. Also, utilize the wealth of knowledge from your own colleagues. Meet with the most technologically-literate person in your school and ask for suggestions! And remain on the look-out for professional development opportunities that can help you to improve your current skills.

 Share:

6. Share your technology ideas with colleagues and ask them for their suggestions.

Part Five: How to Align Teaching and Testing

Teachers should test only what they have taught and in the manner that they have taught it.

 **Reflect:**

1. In a sentence or two, summarize the various testing methods you use in your classroom to assess student learning.

2. Do your tests assess only what you have taught, and in the way you have taught it? Explain.

3. Do you ever include "surprise" items on tests?

✓ **Take Action:**

4. Take one of your existing tests and go through it carefully. Think about how you taught the information, and then assess whether this test aligns with your teaching. Make any necessary revisions.

⟠ **Share:**

5. With your team, discuss the "swimming" example from the book, and relate it to aligning teaching and testing. Then, come up with a list of ways to more closely align teaching and testing.

Part Six: How to Pace Your Lessons Appropriately

Effective instruction involves ensuring that the lesson moves at a quick but **appropriate pace** for learning.

 Reflect:

1. This section of the book includes a list of eight tips for appropriately pacing lessons. Look at the list and reflect on your teaching from the past few days. How many of these tips do you think you are currently using in your own teaching?

2. This section also includes a list of warning signs that your lesson is moving too slowly. Look at this list and reflect on your teaching from the past few days. How many of these warning signs do you think apply to your classroom? Describe which ones could be observed and give examples.

✓ Take Action:

3. Select an upcoming lesson and note your students' behaviors as you teach it. If you observe some of the warning signs, revise your future lesson plans to make the activities more engaging. What were the warning signs, and what will you do differently to address those signs?

🗩 Share:

4. Share with colleagues the eight tips for evaluating pacing. Discuss whether these tips were beneficial to your teaching and your students' learning.

Part Seven: How to Teach Anything to Anyone

This section of the book outlines the five steps that the most effective teachers follow when teaching a new skill or concept.

💡 Reflect:

1. List the five steps to follow when teaching a new skill or concept.

   1.
   2.
   3.
   4.
   5.

2. Do you follow all five steps during each lesson? Explain.

✓ Take Action:

3. Revise an upcoming lesson by improving one or more of the five components discussed in this section.

💬 Share:

4. Share your revised lesson plan with your team and ask for feedback.

Secret Three Summary Checklist

The following statements summarize the strategies from Secret Three. Read each statement and check the column that best represents where you would rank yourself. Reflect on where you can improve.

1 = Rarely or never
2 = Sometimes
3 = On a consistent basis

STRATEGIES	1	2	3
1. I relate the content I teach to the real lives of my students.			
2. I plan my lessons to include hands-on learning and active student involvement.			
3. I differentiate my instruction to meet the various levels of my students.			
4. I am enthusiastic when I am teaching.			
5. My assessments reflect what I have taught in the ways that I have taught it.			
6. My lessons are paced appropriately.			
7. I incorporate technology when appropriate.			
8. As I teach a new skill, I model it for my students.			
9. After I have taught and modeled a skill, I practice it with my students.			
10. I reteach the skills if students are struggling.			
11. I allow for sufficient independent practice of each new skill.			
12. At the end of each lesson, I review with my students by allowing them to demonstrate or explain what they have learned.			

Secret Four:
The Secret of Attitude

Part One: How to Be in Control of Your Attitude: It's Up to You!

One of the main ingredients separating the best teachers from the rest is simply **attitude**.

💡 Reflect:

1. If you were to ask your principal or a colleague to describe your overall attitude, what do you think he or she would say?

2. How do you deal with negative coworkers? Describe your typical response to a chronic complainer.

✓ Take Action:

3. Discuss (with your colleagues) how you feel when working with someone who is always pessimistic. What could be done to help that person change his or her attitude (or what could be done to at least prevent that person from "infecting" others)? Come up with a list of possible solutions.

💬 **Share:**

4. Share your list of solutions with other teachers and administrators as part of an effort to make the school environment more positive.

Part Two: How to Handle Yourself in the Teachers' Lounge

The teachers' lounge should be a place to go and relax for short periods of time during the school day.

💡 Reflect:

1. How would you describe the atmosphere of your teachers' lounge on a typical day?

✓ Take Action:

2. Discuss the teachers' lounge atmosphere with your team. Does everyone perceive the lounge in the same way? Work together as a team to create a more positive environment for your lounge. Implement some of the changes and reevaluate the situation in one month to see if improvements have been made.

💬 Share:

3. Share your team's ideas with all staff to allow them to be part of the efforts to develop a more positive, relaxing atmosphere in the lounge.

Part Three: How to Improve the Attitudes of Your Students

A teacher's **attitude** spills over onto the students and affects their attitudes.

 **Reflect:**

1. This section of the book gives two examples of how teachers might handle an upset student. Think back to a recent event when a student came in from recess, lunch, or another class and was in a bad mood before walking into your classroom. How did you handle the situation?

2. In looking back at the situation, do you think you handled it in an appropriate manner? Explain.

3. Students notice everything about you. Imagine if you asked students to imitate your behaviors. How do you think they would act?

✓ **Take Action:**

4. If you want to improve the way you respond to student behavior, ask a colleague to observe a class period and give you feedback. Or video a lesson and critique your own behaviors. You can improve the way you deal with student misbehavior only if you are aware that there is room to improve!

 **Share:**

5. Make a list of actions and words that can help defuse upset students. Share the list with your colleagues.

Part Four: How to Portray an Attitude of Responsibility

Effective teachers always assume **responsibility** for students who are not succeeding in their classrooms. It doesn't mean it's always their fault, but they look to themselves first.

Reflect:

1. In this part of the book, you read the example of the physician who has many patients dying following surgery, and he blames it on the fact that they are "unhealthy." Is this a surgeon you would want operating on you? By the same token, many teachers immediately blame the students if the students are not learning. Describe your thoughts on this statement. Is it ever true? Why or why not?

✓ Take Action:

2. Even in the classrooms of the most effective teachers, some students have difficulty grasping various concepts. What are some techniques you can use to better help ALL students experience success? Implement the techniques and tweak them over time.

💬 Share:

3. Share your ideas/techniques with colleagues. Ask them to contribute their own ideas. Consider posting the expanded list to your school's internal drive so that all teachers can benefit.

Part Five: How to Defuse Negative Coworkers

In earlier parts of the book and study guide, you were asked to think about the effects of negativity in your school. In this section, you will think about specific steps you can take to defuse a negative coworker.

 **Reflect:**

1. What can you do when …
    (a) A teacher speaks negatively about a student.

    (b) A coworker gripes about something that is happening in the school.

    (c) A coworker gossips about someone at the school—a student, a teacher, a parent, or an administrator.

    (d) A coworker tries to engage you in a power struggle.

Remember that when dealing with the attitudes and actions of those around you, YOU are in control of your response. You can't control what others say or do, but you can control how you respond to them. Always take the right path and walk away from those who are trying to engulf you in negativity.

✓ Take Action:

2. Turn your reflections into a list of strategies and start implementing them immediately.

 Share:

3. Share your strategies with colleagues at school and possibly with an online professional network.

Part Six: How to Have the Best Attitude on the Faculty

A positive attitude is a key element of effective teaching!

💡 Reflect:

1. Who is the most positive person on your faculty? Describe his or her traits.

✓ Take Action:

2. What steps can you take to be more positive in your own teaching?

💬 Share:

3. Ask several positive people (in any field) how they manage to remain so optimistic. Share their answers with colleagues and/or with an online community of educators.

Part Seven: How to Work Cooperatively with Parents

Effective teachers communicate frequently with their students' parents.

💡 Reflect:

1. Do you communicate with parents at the beginning of a new school year? Explain.

2. This section of the book offers advice on dealing with confrontational parents. How have you dealt with a confrontational parent? How might you use the advice in the book? Explain.

✓ Take Action:

3. Make a list of ideas for communicating effectively with parents throughout the year. Include ideas for reaching out to parents at the beginning of the school year, for sending home positive notes periodically, for dealing with confrontational parents, and for working cooperatively with parents on an ongoing basis.

💬 **Share:**

4. Make an effort to be even more effective at letting parents know how much you value their children. Also let them know about the exciting things happening in your classroom. This can be accomplished through phone calls, handwritten notes, a class website, a blog, a newsletter, and/or email!

Secret Four Summary Checklist

The following statements summarize the strategies from Secret Four. Read each statement and check the box that best applies. Wherever you've checked "no," set a goal for yourself to improve in that area.

STRATEGIES	YES	NO
1. I display a positive attitude toward students, colleagues, and parents.		
2. I try to find something positive in all situations.		
3. I try to find ways to improve negative situations.		
4. I bring only positive issues to the teachers' lounge.		
5. I assume personal responsibility for my students' successes and/or struggles.		
6. I don't allow myself to get caught up with negative comments or negative people.		
7. I initiate positive connections with parents.		
8. I let parents know that their child's success is my primary goal.		
9. I avoid gossip.		
10. I model the attitudes and behaviors I'd like to see in my students.		
11. I try to "defuse" negative coworkers rather than add "fuel" to their comments.		

Secret Five:
The Secret of Professionalism

Part One: How and Why to Dress Professionally

Effective teachers act professionally and dress professionally. Thus, their students respect their professionalism.

Reflect:

1. What is the teacher dress code for your school? Does it match your own definition of "professional dress" for teachers?

2. Do you feel that you dress professionally? Explain.

✓ Take Action:

3. Come up with some ways you could model professionalism for students, whether it be through attire or through other avenues if you already dress professionally.

💬 **Share:**

4.   Share your ideas with a few colleagues and possibly with a social media network for teachers.

Part Two: How to "Fit In" Without "Falling In"

The most effective schools promote a sense of family that results in staff camaraderie and a sense of common purpose.

Reflect:

1. The definition of "falling in" is to get caught up with negative people and situations. How could you counsel someone new to your school so that he or she doesn't get caught up with staff members who are less than positive?

2. Effective teachers attract other effective teachers in a school because they have similar outlooks on teaching and learning. Think of the most effective teachers in your school and describe a few of their common qualities.

✓ Take Action:

3. Do you ever try too hard to be accepted? List four or five ways you can get along with others without falling in.

💬 **Share:**

4. This section of the book ends with a list of qualities of effective teachers. Share the list with your colleagues and discuss it.

Part Three: How to Handle Yourself with Social Media

Social media is a wonderful tool if it is used appropriately and professionally.

Reflect:

1. Do you use social media to connect with parents, teachers, or colleagues? If so, how? If not, is this an area you are interested in exploring? Explain.

✓ Take Action:

2. Find out your school's social media policy and, if necessary, suggest revisions or clarifications.

Share:

3. Share, with your team, ideas for better incorporating the use of social media in your school. Be sure to share your school's social media policy with parents so that they are aware of how you are using these tools professionally. And continually remind the students of the dos and don'ts of using social media. Many of them simply don't know!

Part Four: How and Why to Continue Your Professional Growth

Effective teachers (and effective professionals in any field!) never stop learning and growing.

 **Reflect:**

1. The most effective teachers continually look for ways to better their teaching skills and knowledge. Think about a recent workshop or in-service you attended and describe what you gained from it.

2. Do you work to gain knowledge and skills even when your district doesn't expect them or provide them? If so, describe how. If not, describe how you might do this in the future.

3. If you are working through this study guide as part of a professional development plan, you are working to learn the components of being a more effective teacher! Reflect on one of the most important things you have learned thus far. Describe how you intend to use what you have learned.

✓ Take Action:

4. Participate in professional development training that meets your needs in terms of improving content knowledge/delivery, classroom management, integration of technology, etc. This training might be provided by your school/district or through an online or web-based training opportunity.

 ## Share:

5. Share and discuss your answer to #3 with your team or a colleague.

Part Five: How to Bleed Professionalism Without Cutting Yourself

Don't allow your frustrations to rob you of your dignity and your professionalism, regardless of how tempting it may be.

Reflect:

1. It is difficult to always maintain a positive outlook, but effective teachers work hard to do so. What are some of the challenges you've faced during the past week? Describe one challenge and how you dealt with it.

2. Is there anything you wish you had done differently? Explain.

Take Action:

3. List at least two positive actions you can take when confronted with a challenging situation. (Always be prepared to respond to any situation in an appropriate, professional manner.)

💬 Share:

4. Discuss the topic of professionalism with your colleagues and tell what professionalism means to you.

Part Six: How to *Do* Your Best, Not *Be* the Best

The true prize in teaching comes from touching a student's life.

Reflect:

1. This section of the book incorporates quotes from several teachers about portraying a positive attitude, growing professionally, and maintaining high levels of enthusiasm. Reread these quotes and select one to which you can relate. Summarize your choice, telling why you selected it.

2. Though we all want to do our best and be our best, we don't always succeed. Regarding doing your best in teaching, choose one area you feel you could improve upon, and list it here.

✓ Take Action:

3. Focus on the one area you selected in question 2 for the next week. At the end of the week, reflect on the changes that have occurred as a result of your efforts.

 Share:

4. Discuss your efforts with one or more of your colleagues.

Part Seven: How to Make Decisions That Benefit Children

Effective teachers make their decisions based on what is best for students.

 **Reflect:**

1. This part of the chapter provides examples of two very different schools. In which school would you prefer to teach? Why?

2. Which of the two schools best matches the one in which you teach? Explain.

✓ **Take Action:**

3. Record this question on an index card, sticky note, tablet, or smart phone: "Is this what's best for my students or easiest for me?" Refer to it often as you make decisions. Tape a copy of it on the top of your desk!

💬 **Share:**

4. Share with colleagues some ideas about how you can all make decisions (at the classroom level and at the school level) that better benefit students.

Secret Five Summary Checklist

The following statements summarize the strategies from Secret Five. Read each statement and check the column that best represents where you would rank yourself. Reflect on where you can improve.

1 = Rarely or never
2 = Sometimes
3 = On a consistent basis

STRATEGIES	1	2	3
1. I conduct myself as a professional.			
2. I dress professionally.			
3. I seek out other positive coworkers and align myself with them.			
4. I maintain control of myself in all situations in my classroom.			
5. I don't take students' misbehavior personally.			
6. I maintain a calm voice in all situations.			
7. I attack the problem as opposed to the person.			
8. I participate in professional development activities.			
9. I always strive to do my best, as opposed to trying to be the best.			
10. I keep my students as my main focus.			

Secret Six:
The Secret of Effective Discipline

Part One: How to Hide Your Buttons from Your Students

When you allow students to push your buttons, you give away your control.

💡 Reflect:

1. This section of the book uses the example of pressing a button on an elevator to illustrate what students try to do to teachers on a daily basis. Do you have buttons that you allow your students to push? What is your hottest button?

2. Ask yourself these questions and carefully consider your answers.
   (a) Do students know when they get to me?

   (b) Can they tell that I am aggravated?

   (c) What do I look like when I become aggravated, upset, or frustrated with my students?

✓ Take Action:

3. Reread the suggestions for hiding your buttons from your students. Add to the list and revise any ones that don't work for you.

💬 Share:

4. Share your list with your colleagues and develop a combined list of ways to hide your buttons from your students.

Part Two: How to Be Consistent with Discipline

One of the best-kept secrets of the most effective teachers is that they have very few discipline problems.

⚡ Reflect:

1. List the two things (shared in this section of the book) that effective teachers have in common with regard to discipline. Do you do these two things? If not, how can you improve?

2. Does your school have a building-wide discipline plan? Explain.

3. Is your discipline plan and/or the school plan consistently enforced? Explain.

✓ **Take Action:**

4. How might you involve students in the development of the class rules next year? Come up with two ways to accomplish that.

⟲ **Share:**

5. Share your plan with colleagues and ask how they involve students in creating their own rules.

Part Three: How to Relieve Stress with Psychology

The most effective teachers are the ones who seem to be the least stressed and to have the fewest discipline problems.

 **Reflect:**

1. This part of the book offers two examples of how teachers can use positive techniques to deal with students who are off-task. Have you ever used a similar technique? Describe what you have done. If not, describe how you might use one in the future.

2. This section also lists several statements that effective teachers use when working with students. Can you add other examples of complimentary statements?

✓ **Take Action:**

3. Practice using some of the complimentary statements in class! How does it feel?

💬 Share:

4. Discuss the list of complimentary phrases with your team members, and add as many as you can. This list can never be long enough!

Part Four: How to Become Better, Not Bitter

The most effective teachers choose the better, as opposed to the bitter, path.

 **Reflect:**

1. Unfortunately, bitter teachers reside in most schools. You probably know a few. List a few of their "common phrases."

✓ **Take Action:**

2. Come up with two ways to turn a negative situation into a positive learning opportunity.

💬 **Share:**

3. Share your two ways (from question 2) with colleagues and ask them to share theirs with you. When you find yourself in a situation where you could go either way, talk about it with a trusted colleague—but not a negative one!

Part Five: How to Give Students What They Want and Need

If you want to know what students want and need—ask them!

 **Reflect:**

1. This part of the book begins with a list of what students want and need from their teachers. Ask your own students what they want and need from YOU. Record their statements.

 **Take Action:**

2. Summarize your students' feedback, and use it to develop your own "Teacher's Creed." Display it in your classroom.

⏵ **Share:**

3. Share with your colleagues the "Teacher's Creed" you developed. Consider collaborating on a "Teachers' Creed" for the entire school.

Part Six: How to Be Self-Disciplined

If you can't control yourself, you'll never control a group of students!

⚲ Reflect:

1. This section of the book describes two very different reactions to a student's misbehavior. Which reaction can you relate to the most? Explain.

2. Ms. Rattleless didn't get into a power struggle with Amy in front of the class. Is that easy to do? Explain.

3. Why was Ms. Fuse Box's approach unsuccessful?

4. What were the key strategies Ms. Rattleless used in dealing with Amy's outburst?

✓ Take Action:

5. Start a log of how you handle yourself during difficult situations in the classroom. For each situation, tell what happened and how you reacted. When appropriate, think of a way you could have handled the situation better and record that in your log.

 Share:

6. Share your list with a trusted colleague and solicit ideas for maintaining control in ANY situation. Again, seek a positive colleague for this activity.

Part Seven: How to Find the Good in Every Child

Students who feel good about themselves are much less likely to misbehave than those who do not.

💡 Reflect:

1. Teachers are trained to look for problems their students are having: reading deficiencies, behavior problems, special education issues, and so forth. On the flip side, teachers are not always trained to look for the *good* in children. As you look around your class, can you identify the good qualities in EVERY student? Describe some of the good qualities that you have recognized in your students.

2. One example cited in the book was from a teacher who used an *interest inventory* to get to know her students better. List two other ways teachers can get to know their students. Name two ways of helping your students get to know you better.

✓ Take Action:

3. Come up with a plan for getting to know your students better this year. Keep it simple, but do it. It's vital that you get to know your students if you're going to be effective.

💬 Share:

4. Ask students to share their personal interests not only with you but with the whole class, via a class project, an interest inventory, pictures, a bulletin board display, an online class page, etc.

Secret Six Summary Checklist

The following statements summarize the strategies from Secret Six. Read each statement and check the column that best represents where you would rank yourself. Reflect on where you can improve.

1 = Rarely or never
2 = Sometimes
3 = On a consistent basis

STRATEGIES	1	2	3
1. In all school situations, I appear calm and in control.			
2. I have a specific discipline plan that I follow consistently.			
3. I avoid arguing with my students or engaging in power struggles.			
4. I use psychology to ward off potential problems.			
5. I ask my students what they want, need, and expect in my classroom.			
6. I have a Teacher's Creed displayed in my classroom.			
7. I work hard at choosing to be better, not bitter.			
8. I work at identifying what's "good" in each of my students.			

Secret Seven:
The Secret of Motivation
and Inspiration

Part One: How to Make *Your* Excitement *Their* Excitement

We remember two groups of teachers: the really good ones and the really bad ones!

Reflect:

1. Reflect on the best teacher you ever had. Describe what that teacher did to earn that recognition from you.

2. Now describe the habits and actions of the worst teacher you ever had.

3. Is your classroom "Sunny and Bright" or "Cloudy and Dreary"? Or is it a mix? Explain.

4. Do you possess the same characteristics that you described in question 1? Why or why not?

✓ Take Action:

5. Keep a list of the characteristics of your favorite teacher on your desk. Refer to it often. Be that teacher! Remind yourself, every day, that you set the mood in your classroom.

 Share:

6. Gather with colleagues and share your ideas of what a "Sunny and Bright" classroom should look like.

Part Two: How to Make Every Student Feel Like Your Favorite Student

All students want and deserve to feel just as valued as every other student in the classroom.

💡 Reflect:

1. This section of the book begins with an effective teacher discussing why and how she tries to make each student feel special. If you were asked the same question, what would your answer be?

2. Effective teachers make genuinely positive comments such as welcoming students to the classroom and praising those who behave as expected. Provide examples of how you use positive comments in your daily interactions with students.

3. This section also offers examples of anonymous praise and anonymous fussing. Which example best describes you and your interactions with your students? Explain.

✓ Take Action:

4. For the next three days, use the approach of anonymous praise and see how your students respond. Reflect on the results.

🗩 Share:

5. Share with your colleagues your own ways of making every student feel like your favorite.

Part Three: How to Show Personal Interest in Every Student

One of the best ways to motivate and inspire students is to show personal interest in them.

Reflect:

1. Do you have any students about whom you know very little? What could you do to get to know them better?

2. List two ways you show students that they are important to you.

3. What advice would you give to a new teacher regarding the importance of showing personal interest in students—especially those who struggle?

✓ Take Action:

4. Identify two students who are struggling—either with personal or academic issues. Make those two your project for the next two weeks. Make an extra effort to show personal interest in them and to make them feel valued.

 Share:

5. Share your experiences (with those two students) with your colleagues. Continue to show personal interest in those students. And now do the same with two more. And two more!

Part Four: How to Maximize the Power of Praise

Effective teachers agree that praise is one of the most powerful tools we can use to positively impact our students.

💡 Reflect:

1. This part of the book uses the word SUCCESS to illustrate the components of praise and how it should be incorporated into your daily habits and routines. Think of times you have praised your students in the past week.
    (a) Was your praise specific? Give examples. If not, how could you have made it more specific?

    (b) Was your praise unconditional, credible, and enthusiastic? Explain.

    (c) Do you use praise consistently? How?

    (d) How much enthusiasm do you put into the praise?

(e) Are you able to give praise as a "stand alone" and not link it to other behaviors of the students? Give an example of "stand alone" praise in your classroom.

(f) Is the praise you are giving to students in line with their abilities and expectations? Think about the praise you recently gave a student and determine if it was suitable for that student.

✓ Take Action:

2. Starting tomorrow, praise your students, keeping in mind the tips discussed in this section. Note how students react.

⬭ **Share:**

3. Through an in-person or online discussion with other teachers, share several ways you use praise effectively in your classroom.

Part Five: How to Use Rewards Appropriately

The real secret to using rewards in the classroom is not *if* you use them but if you use them **effectively**.

💡 Reflect:

1. Reflect on the "Quarterly Challenge" example in this chapter. In your own words, why wasn't it effective?

2. Has your school ever tried such a program? Was it successful? Explain.

3. Do you have a reward system in your classroom and/or school? Describe it briefly.

✓ **Take Action:**

4. Talk to two or three effective teachers and ask them to share how they use both praise and rewards. Try some of their ideas.

🗩 **Share:**

5. The next time you meet with your team, discuss your ideas, successes, and struggles with using rewards and praise.

Part Six: How to Motivate Unmotivated Students

Effective teachers find ways to motivate *all* students.

💡 Reflect:

1. This section of the book includes statements from effective teachers and less-than-effective teachers regarding student motivation. What is the main difference in the two groups?

2. What are some motivational strategies that you have used to get your students interested in their learning?

✓ Take Action:

3. Read an article, join in an online discussion, or ask a colleague for a few ideas for increasing student motivation. Try one or two of the ideas in your classroom.

4. Ask your students what motivates them to learn. Compile their suggestions. Note any similarities to the list discussed on page 133 in the book.

🗩 Share:

5. Share the student motivation list with your colleagues and ask them to share their own secrets for motivating students.

Part Seven: How to Maximize the Power of YOU

How you feel about yourself helps to determine how you treat your students.

💡 Reflect:

1. As we reach the end of this study guide, what impact have the reflections and discussions had on you and your teaching?

2. This section of the book deals with YOU and how you can stay positive as you teach the students who have been entrusted to your care. Refer to the list of eight tips other effective teachers use to stay positive. Do you use any of these? Explain.

✓ Take Action:

3. List three strategies you use to help yourself remain positive, even when you have to fake it.

💬 Share:

4. Discuss with your colleagues the importance of serving as a positive role model for your students. Share any suggestions you have for keeping a positive, professional demeanor—especially on those days when you don't feel positive.

Secret Seven Summary Checklist

The following statements summarize the strategies from Secret Seven. Read each statement and check the column that best represents where you would rank yourself. Reflect on where you can improve.

1 = Rarely or never
2 = Sometimes
3 = On a consistent basis

STRATEGIES	1	2	3
1. I appear excited and motivated in my classroom.			
2. I show personal interest in my students.			
3. I try to make all students feel like my favorite.			
4. I provide specific praise when earned.			
5. I provide unconditional praise when earned.			
6. I provide praise on a consistent basis to promote positive behaviors.			
7. I don't compromise praise by including a negative statement.			
8. I use rewards effectively in the classroom.			
9. I continually search for new ways to motivate my students.			
10. I remind myself often that I am in this profession because I want to have a positive influence on my students' lives.			

Conclusion

The choice to be an effective teacher is yours. You now possess the seven simple secrets of effective teachers. Take that knowledge and use it! Use it to motivate, to inspire, to challenge, and to positively influence every student you teach.

The ideas, activities, suggestions, and strategies in *Seven Simple Secrets* and in this study guide were designed to provide a foundation to help you build your own blueprint for success. You're now well on your way to becoming your very best self. Your students deserve nothing less.

> Remember, teachers, that your influence is powerful. Be it positive or negative, it is lasting. You will live in the hearts of your students long after you are gone from this earth.

BONUS Seven!

This section of the main book features seven lists that can be photocopied or downloaded, http://www.routledge.com/books/details/9781138013735/. The following are suggestions for using the lists:

1. First, and most importantly, use these lists in your own classroom!

2. Choose one or more of the lists to share during . . .

   + full staff meetings
   + team or department meetings
   + meetings with your mentor or closest colleagues
   + book studies
   + sessions with your PLC

3. Take an item from one of the lists and start a discussion about it on your favorite social media site.

4. Choose an item from one of the lists and extend your learning by researching the topic online and reading more about it.

5. Post one or more of the lists in your teachers' lounge to inspire others.

6. Read the list of "Seven Things Effective Teachers Don't Do" once a week or once a month and ask yourself whether you are avoiding these things.

7. Paste the "Seven Things Effective Teachers Do Every Day" in a prominent place so that you see it every day.

8. Come up with your own top seven list and share it with others!